GREGORY L. VOGT

EARTH

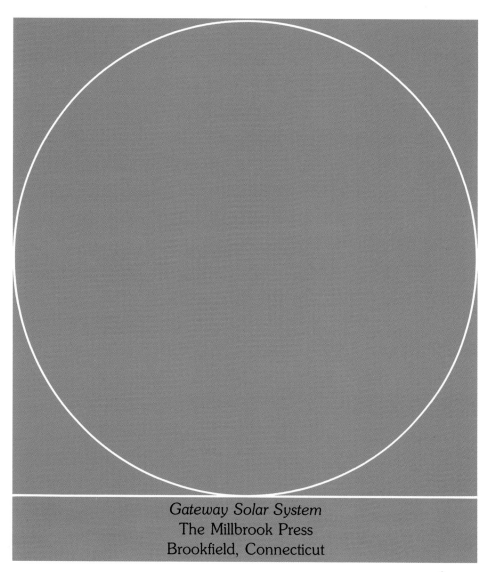

Gateway Solar System
The Millbrook Press
Brookfield, Connecticut

All photographs courtesy of NASA

Library of Congress Cataloging-in-Publication Data
Vogt, Gregory.
Earth / Gregory L. Vogt.
p.   cm.
Includes bibliographical references and index.
Summary: Presents information on the geology,
atmosphere, seasons,
and orbit of planet Earth.
ISBN 1-56294-602-1 (lib. bdg.)
1. Earth—Juvenile literature.   2. Moon—Juvenile literature.
[1. Earth.]   I. Title.
QB631.4.V63   1996
550—dc20   95-19738   CIP   AC

Published by The Millbrook Press, Inc.
2 Old New Milford Road
Brookfield, Connecticut 06804

EARTH

Earth rises above the Moon's horizon. This picture was taken by the crew of Apollo 8 in 1968.

Liftoff!

It is hard to imagine what Frank Borman, James A. Lovell, and William A. Anders felt when the seats of their Apollo command module suddenly slammed into their backs. Rising up on a pillar of flame, a giant Saturn V rocket carried the three into space. They weren't the first men to travel into space, but they did do something that no other astronauts had done. After a final thrust from the rocket's third stage, they rode their Apollo 8 spacecraft to the Moon and back. It was a test mission, which would lead to the first landing on the Moon seven months later.

The nose of their spacecraft pointed into space, and the three men watched the Moon grow larger as they coasted toward it. Nearly three days after leaving Earth, Borman, Lovell, and Anders saw a sight no human had seen before. As their spacecraft rounded the far side of the Moon, a small glimmer of color separated the blackness of space from the stark, cratered gray surface of the Moon. The glimmer grew larger and rounder and finally stood alone as a brilliant blue, white, and brownish sphere. Earth had risen above the Moon's *horizon*.

From lunar *orbit*, some 238,600 miles (384,000 kilometers) away, the men were amazed at how alone and how fragile Earth appeared. Lovell, in radio transmissions to Mission Control in Houston, called Earth a "grand oasis in the big vastness of space."

Earth isn't a very large planet. It has a diameter of 7,926 miles (12,756 kilometers) at its *equator* and a slightly smaller diameter—26 miles (42 kilometers) less—between its poles. The rapid rotation of Earth, approximately once every 24 hours, causes the equatorial region, or mid-region, of the sphere to bulge slightly, just as a water-filled balloon bulges at its middle when it is spun in the air.

A Planet Called Earth?

When seen from outer space, Earth doesn't seem to have the right name. It should probably be called "Planet Water." Seventy percent of its surface is covered with oceans averaging about 2.5 miles (4 kilometers) deep. Only 30 percent of Earth's surface is actually earth, or land.

Another possible name for Earth might be "Planet Life," because it is the only planet in the Sun's *solar system* that is known to be a home for living things. On and in Earth's land, in its water and air, and even in its ice, snow, and hot springs are millions of species of plants, animals, and microorganisms. After living on Earth for billions of years, they have gradually adapted

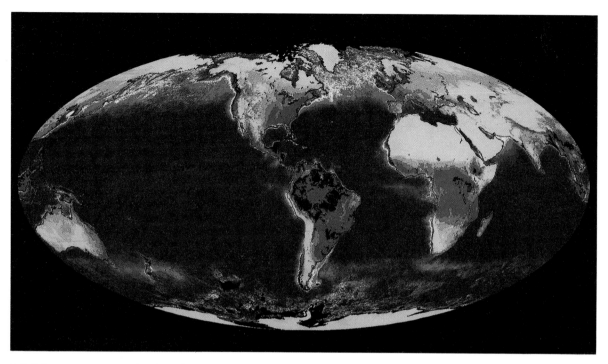

NASA scientists study the different environments in which plants and animals live on Earth by using photographs taken by an Earth satellite and colored by computers. In this map, the colors in the ocean and on land show how much plant life thrives in each area.

so that they interact with each other and with the land, water, and air in a fragile yet enduring *ecosystem*. Within this system, chemicals and energy are continually traded, or cycled, between the living and nonliving parts of Earth.

Earth is a very suitable home for living things. Its distance from the Sun, about 93 million miles (149.6 million kilometers), is just right. Water, which is essential to living things, is liquid only in temperatures between

32 and 212 degrees Fahrenheit (0 and 100 degrees Celsius). If Earth were much closer to the Sun, its water would boil away. If it were farther away, all the water would freeze solid. At its perfect distance, Earth gets the right amount of sunlight to enable plants to grow, and the plants provide food for the animals.

Shell of Air

Earth has a protective *atmosphere* of gas that shields the planet's surface from deadly space *radiation*. When Earth is seen from space, its atmosphere gives the planet some of its bluish look. White sunlight actually contains a rainbow of colors. When sunlight enters the atmosphere, some of its blue color is scattered. This gives the sky a bluish look, whether you look at the atmosphere from Earth's surface or from outer space.

Although dense enough to support life on Earth, the atmosphere looks thin when its thickness is compared to the size of the planet. If Earth were the same size as a peach, its atmosphere would be as thick as the fuzz on the peach's skin. This surrounding envelope of air is made up mostly of the gases nitrogen (78 percent) and oxygen (21 percent), but also contains small amounts of argon, neon, carbon dioxide, water vapor, and a special heavy form of oxygen called *ozone*.

As you can see in this photo taken by NASA astronauts on the Skylab space station in 1973, the atmosphere surrounding Earth is only a thin layer of blue.

Scientists have divided Earth's atmosphere into layers. The layers differ from each other in their temperatures, the amounts of air present, and the things that happen there. Nearest Earth's surface is the *troposphere,* where the events we call *weather* take place. Above the troposphere is the *stratosphere,* where high-flying jet planes travel. Above that is the *mesosphere,* or middle atmosphere, where dangerous radiation, such as ultraviolet light, is filtered. And still higher is the *thermosphere,* where the air is very thin and where Earth-

9

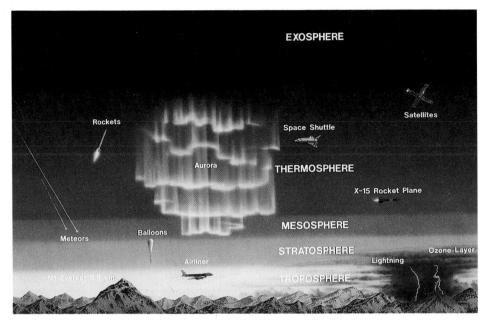

Scientists have divided Earth's atmosphere into layers. Each layer has different air and temperature characteristics.

orbiting spacecraft, like space shuttles, travel. Finally, there is the *exosphere,* or outer space, which is home to the Moon as well as to the other planets, *comets, meteors,* and *asteroids.*

Planetary Heat Engine

Powered by sunlight, Earth's atmosphere works like a great engine that moves moisture across Earth's surface and balances its cold and warm temperatures.

Sunlight warms the land. It also warms the air

above the land. The warm air rises, because warm air is lighter than cool air, and winds of cool air move in to replace it. This cool air gradually warms and rises, too.

While rising, the warm air currents carry water vapor that has *evaporated* from rivers, lakes, oceans, and plants. High up in the atmosphere, the rising column of warm air starts to cool and spread over Earth's surface. As the air cools, the water condenses into tiny droplets to form clouds. The clouds shade parts of Earth's surface from the Sun's warmth. As more water vapor is carried upward, the droplets in the cooled air eventually become heavy and fall back to Earth as rain or snow. This movement of water up into the atmosphere and back down onto the land is one of Earth's important cycles.

In addition to Earth's atmospheric engine, a great engine is at work within Earth's oceans. The greatest part of the Sun's energy falls on the area near the equator and warms the water there the most. Cooler water to the north and south sinks to the ocean depths, and warm water from the equatorial regions spreads across the surface to replace it. These movements of cold and warm water are called *currents*. They help distribute the Sun's warmth throughout the planet. Wind, driven by the Sun's energy, creates the waves that crisscross the world's ocean basins and lap the shores of continents.

The Seasons

As Earth orbits the Sun, a journey that takes 365.25 days to complete, there are wide shifts in weather patterns. These are the *seasons,* and they are caused not by Earth's distance from the Sun but by the tilt of Earth's *axis.*

The axis is an imaginary line drawn through the middle of Earth from the North Pole to the South Pole. Earth spins on this axis. The axis is tilted at an angle of 23.5 degrees to Earth's orbit. When it is summer in Earth's Northern Hemisphere, the North Pole end of the axis leans toward the Sun. Because of this, the Northern Hemisphere gets more hours of daylight in summer than it does in winter, the Sun climbs higher in the sky, and the days are hotter.

While the Northern Hemisphere is experiencing summer, the Southern Hemisphere is experiencing winter, because the South Pole end of Earth's axis is tilted away from the Sun. The days are shorter, and the Sun sinks lower in the sky, which makes the days colder. Six months later, when Earth is on the other side of the Sun, the South Pole axis leans more toward the Sun than the North Pole end does. Then it is summer in the Southern Hemisphere and winter in the Northern Hemisphere.

A Jigsaw Puzzle

The most magnificent part of Earth, when it is viewed from space, are the continents. Seen from the vicinity of the Moon, the continents appear mostly brownish, but seen close up, from a space-shuttle orbit, many colors stand out brilliantly. The rocks and soil of Earth appear

This photograph from the space shuttle STS-54 shows the different textures and colors of the Sahara Desert in North Africa, which contains both sand dunes and mountains.

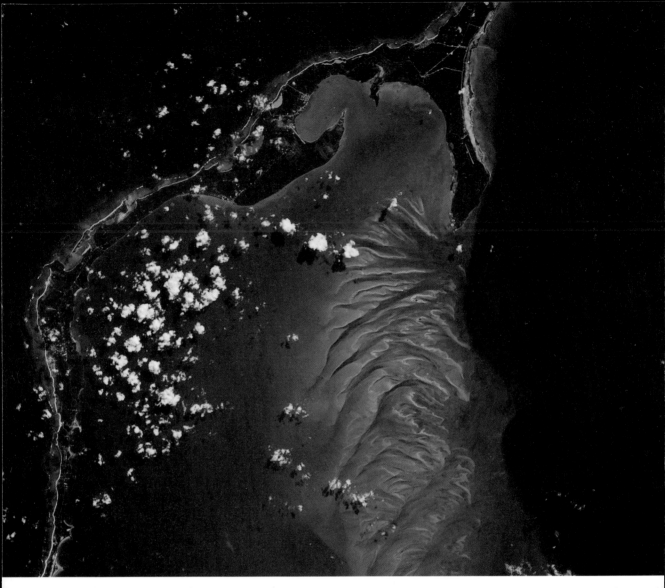

In the shallow waters of the Atlantic Ocean, a network of sandbars and sand channels forms Eleuthera Island in the Bahamas.

white, brown, yellow, red, and black, and plants covering the surface take on every shade of green. The snow and ice are bright white because they reflect sunlight so strongly.

Perhaps what is most remarkable about the continents when viewed from space is their jigsaw-puzzle appearance. Scientists have long wondered if all the continents were once joined in Earth's distant past. If you look at a globe, you can see that the eastern coastlines of North and South America and the western coastlines of Europe and Africa have similar shapes. It's as though they were the matching pieces of a giant jigsaw puzzle. The island of Madagascar, in the Indian Ocean, looks as if it had been broken off the eastern coast of Africa. Australia could easily fit into the shoreline gap where the Indian Ocean is located.

In this computer-drawn picture of Earth, it is easy to see the way Europe, Africa, and North and South America once fit together like a giant jigsaw puzzle.

In addition to the shapes of the continents, scientists have had other clues in this jigsaw-puzzle mystery. If all the water in Earth's oceans could be drained away, you would see a branching mountain chain, 40,000 miles (64,000 kilometers) long, running along the ocean floor. The chain is in the center of the Atlantic Ocean and almost exactly parallels the outlines of the continents. There are more mountain chains on the Pacific Ocean side of the continents, and the land there is wracked by earthquakes and volcanic eruptions.

Putting these clues together, scientists now believe that Earth's continents were joined as one supercontinent more than 200 million years ago. Scientists discovered this by investigating Earth's interior. By measuring the vibrations created by earthquake waves as they pass through Earth, scientists have learned that Earth's interior, like its atmosphere, is layered.

In the center, there is an *inner core* of solid nickel and iron. This is surrounded by an *outer core* of molten nickel and iron metal. Above the core is a *mantle* of rock, which in some places is so hot and under so much pressure that it flows slowly. Above the mantle is the outer layer, or *crust,* which is about 6 miles (10 kilometers) thick under the oceans and as much as 30 miles (50 kilometers) thick under the continents. The crust is broken into large pieces, or *plates,* that float on the mantle beneath them.

When the solar system formed more than 4 billion years ago, Earth was very hot and molten. In time it began to cool, and its surface hardened. (Earth continues to cool even today.) Heat from the interior causes the soft mantle to flow in currents. The currents push the plates very slowly. Because of this, North America is moving into the Pacific Basin about as fast as your fingernails grow. This movement creates great friction when the continental plates collide with the Pacific Ocean plates. The leading edges of the ocean plates are driven under the continental plates. The western regions of the continents slowly crumple and fold and create high mountain ranges. Sudden breaks in the rocks miles below the surface create earthquakes. Hot lava works its way upward through the cracks and erupts and flows over the surface of the land.

Building Up, Tearing Down, and Building Up Again

As the land is lifted up and formed into mountains by forces acting on Earth's crust, it is also being torn down. Wind, rain, ice, chemicals, and even plants and animals erode, or wear away, the slowly rising rock. The rock is at first broken into large angular blocks that tumble down mountain slopes and crack into smaller pieces. Fast-flowing rivers and slow-moving glaciers or rivers of ice carry the rock and grind it down further, rounding its edges. As the rivers spread out over the continents, the speed of the water lessens. Water collects in depressions and forms lakes. Eventually, boulders from the mountain peaks first become pebbles and then *sediment* (sand and clay).

Some of the sediment becomes soil in which trees, grass, and flowers anchor themselves to grow. Other sediment works its way through rivers and settles in ocean basins. In time, sediments accumulate in the

In 1994, astronauts on the space shuttle saw the swirling clouds of hurricane Florence.

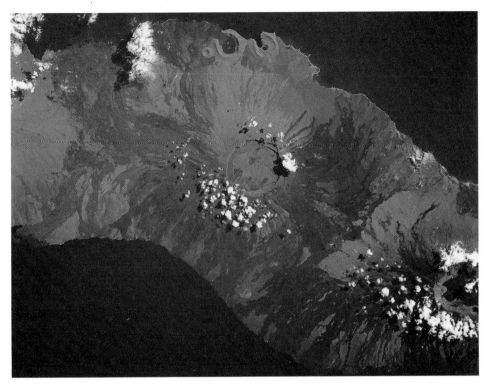
Photos taken by space shuttles helped scientists see clearly that Isabela in the Galapagos Islands was built up by lava flows (the dark areas) from a now inactive volcano.

oceans and fuse together to form new rock. In perhaps hundreds of millions of years, movements in the crust push up the rock and create new mountains.

In a very slow but constant cycle, Earth's land is built up, worn down, and built up again. The land cycle is another of the many interacting cycles that shape Earth and make it the most diverse and fascinating planet in the solar system.

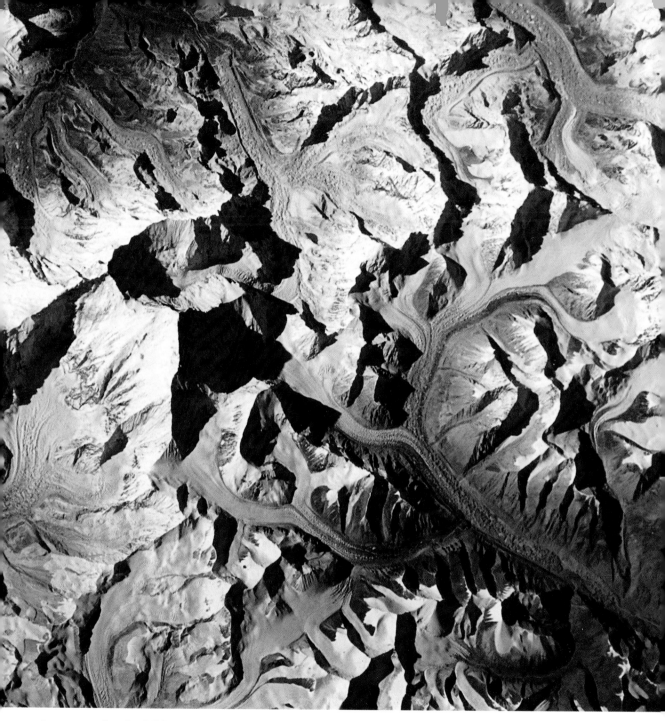

As space shuttle STS-66 astronauts flew over Mount Everest, the world's highest mountain, they could see how slow-moving glaciers are carving deep valleys into the rocky land.

The flight of Apollo 8 was one of nine Apollo missions to the Moon. On six of those flights, teams of two astronauts, each protected inside a bulky white space suit, landed on the Moon and spent many hours exploring the lunar surface. By the time the crew of Apollo 17, the last mission, landed back on Earth, scientists had 843 pounds (382 kilograms) of Moon rock and sedi-

Over millions of years, the water of the Colorado River eroded the land and created what is now the Grand Canyon. The white areas in the photo are snow.

ment to analyze. One of their many goals in studying lunar material was to find out where the Moon came from.

The Moon is Earth's nearest neighbor in space. It is a rocky world some 2,160 miles (3,476 kilometers) in diameter. It orbits Earth at an average distance of 238,600 miles (384,000 kilometers) and circles once in just over 27 days.

Here Apollo 11 astronaut Edwin E. ("Buzz") Aldrin prepares a group of scientific instruments that will be left on the Moon to gather more information for scientists back on Earth.

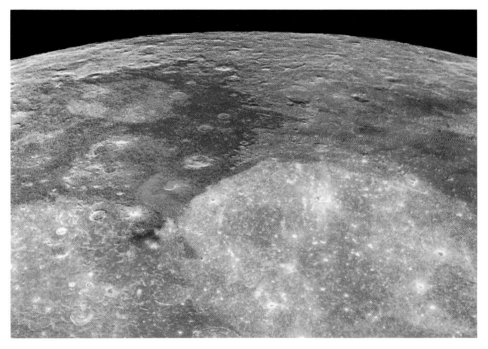

NASA's Galileo spacecraft flew past the Moon in 1992 and took many pictures of the Moon's surface. This photograph was colored by computer to make craters and other important details of the surface easier to see. Sediment on the Moon that is rich in the element titanium is colored blue. Sediment with less titanium is orange.

Because of their closeness to each other, the combined gravitational forces of Earth and Moon have locked the Moon into one position. So, as the Moon orbits, it always has the same side turned toward Earth. Through a telescope, you can see that the Moon's near side is pocked with craters, dotted with mountain ranges, and scattered with broad basins that resemble seas. The color of the surface is light to dark gray. When the Apollo 8 crew circled the far side of the Moon, they observed many more craters of all sizes, overlapping craters, and mountains, but they found no broad basins like those on the side facing Earth.

Rock samples brought back from the Moon helped scientists confirm some of the theories they had about the Moon's origin. The craters are the result of the impact of millions of *meteorites,* or space rocks, of all sizes,

Apollo 11 astronauts Neil A. Armstrong and Edwin E. Aldrin are leaving the Moon and are on their way home to Earth.

which slammed into the Moon and blasted holes in its surface. The basins on the Moon's near side are the result of the ancient collisions of much larger space rocks called *asteroids*. About 3 to 4 billion years ago, the floors of these basins were filled with volcanic basalt lava that flowed out onto the Moon's surface.

From studying these Moon rocks and other evidence, many scientists now think that the Moon is the offspring of Earth and a planet that no longer exists. They believe that in the very earliest days of Earth, some 4.5 billion years ago, a rocky world about the size of Mars (4,222 miles, or 6,794 kilometers, in diameter) collided with the molten Earth. The force of the impact shattered the rocky world, creating a cloud of debris. The debris collected into disklike rings much like those surrounding the planet Saturn. Soon afterward, the debris clumped together and formed our Moon.

The Future

One reason scientists study our Earth and Moon is to try to learn what these two bodies in our solar system will become in the future. It is likely that millions or billions of years from now, Earth and Moon will fall into each other and become one body in space. Long before that happens, however, other disasters may befall Earth. The

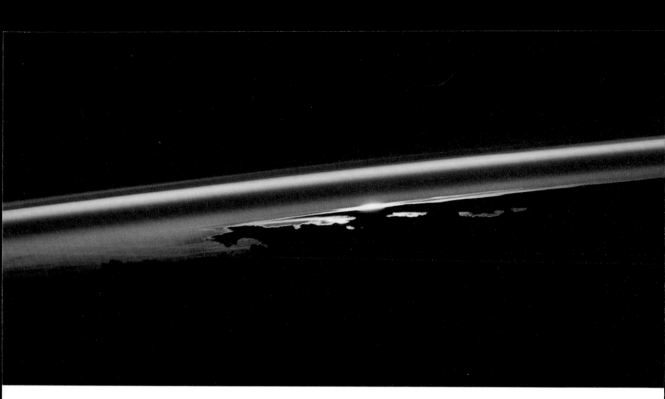

The tops of thunderclouds cast beautiful shadows as the astronauts on space shuttle STS-47 watched the sunset from Earth's orbit.

greatest of these potential disasters might be caused by humankind's altering of the planet. In the short time we have been on Earth, we have pushed many life-forms into extinction, laid waste millions of acres of forest and prairie, and polluted our oceans and air.

We often forget that Earth is our only home. Our study of the solar system teaches us that no other planet offers the resources, diverse environments, or beauty that our Earth does. If we continue to damage our home, it could someday become unfit for human life. If that happens, we will soon discover that there is no other place to go.

EARTH QUICK FACTS

Earth: Name derived from words in several languages such as *erthe* (Middle English), *eorthe* (Old English), *jǫrth* (Old Norse), and *airtha* (Gothic).

Average Distance from the Sun
Millions of miles   93,000,000
Millions of kilometers   149,600,000

Revolution (one orbit around the Sun)   365.25 days

Average Orbital Speed
Miles per second   18.6
Kilometers per second   30

Rotation (spinning once)   23 hours 56 minutes

Diameter at Equator
Miles   7,926
Kilometers   12,756

Surface Gravity   32 feet (9.8 meters) per second^2

Mass (the amount of matter)
Pounds   132 (followed by 22 zeros)
Kilograms   6 (followed by 23 zeros)

Earth's Moon	Diameter	Distance from Planet
Miles	2,160	238,600
Kilometers	3,476	384,000

GLOSSARY

Asteroid	A large rocky body, smaller than a planet, that orbits the Sun
Atmosphere	The collection of gases that surrounds a planet
Axis	An imaginary line running from the north to the south pole of a planet
Comet	A small icy body that orbits the Sun and produces a tail of gas and dust when it is warmed by the Sun's heat
Crust	The outer solid layer of Earth
Currents	Streams of water flowing within oceans
Ecosystem	A community of plants, animals, microorganisms, air, water, soil, and energy that interact and support each other in nature
Equator	An imaginary line circling a planet halfway between its north and south poles
Evaporation	The process by which liquids turn into gas
Exosphere	The outermost layer of Earth's atmosphere
Horizon	The farthest edge of Earth you can see
Inner Core	The solid innermost layer of Earth
Mantle	A thick, slowly flowing layer of Earth lying between the outer core and the crust
Mesosphere	The middle layer of Earth's atmosphere
Meteor	A speck of comet dust that burns up and glows when it enters Earth's atmosphere
Meteorite	A piece of space rock or metal that collides with the surface of a planet or moon
Orbit	The path the Moon takes to travel around Earth or a planet around its sun
Outer Core	A liquid layer of Earth's interior lying between the inner core and the mantle

Ozone	A special molecule of oxygen that contains three atoms of oxygen rather than the usual two
Plates	Large pieces of Earth's crust that support Earth's continents and ocean basins and float about on the mantle like rafts
Radiation	Energy, such as radio waves, visible light, and X rays, that travels through space
Seasons	Annual shifts in Earth's weather due to the inclination of Earth's axis with respect to the Sun
Sediment	An accumulation of rock particles
Solar System	The Sun and its family of planets, moons, asteroids, comets, and meteors
Stratosphere	The layer of Earth's atmosphere lying between the troposphere and mesosphere
Thermosphere	The thin outer layer of Earth's atmosphere
Troposphere	The layer of Earth's atmosphere next to Earth's surface
Weather	Events that take place in Earth's troposphere, such as wind, rain, and temperature changes

FOR FURTHER READING

Brewer, Duncan. *Planet Earth and The Universe.* New York: Marshall Cavendish, 1992.

Fradin, Dennis B. *Earth.* Chicago: Childrens Press, 1989.

Gallant, Roy A. *Our Universe.* Washington, D.C.: National Geographic Society, 1986.

Jennings, Terry, J. *The Earth.* New York: Marshall Cavendish, 1988.

Lauber, Patricia. *Seeing Earth From Space.* New York: Orchard Books, 1990.

INDEX

ABOUT THE AUTHOR

Gregory L. Vogt works for NASA's Education Division
at the Johnson Space Center in Houston, Texas.
He works with astronauts in developing educational
videos for schools.

Mr. Vogt previously served as the executive director of the
Discovery World Museum of Science, Economics and
Technology in Milwaukee, Wisconsin, and as an eighth-
grade science teacher. He holds bachelor's and master's
degrees in science from the University of Wisconsin at
Milwaukee, as well as a doctorate in curriculum and
instruction from Oklahoma State University.